Book Title:

"Advanced Frugal Living: 25 More Tips for Saving Money and Increasing Productivity"

Frugal Living and Productivity Tips: Volume 2

By Jenny Koo

Imprint: Independently published.

Copyright © 2024 by Jenny K. Koo. All rights reserved.

No part of this book may be used or reproduced in any manner whatsoever without written permission.

For information, please email to
jennykookk@gmail.com

Table of Contents

Introduction
- Revisiting the Importance of Frugal Living
- Expanding Your Frugal and Productive Habits
- What You'll Learn in This Volume

Chapter 1: Creative DIY Projects
1. Tip 1
2. Tip 2
3. Tip 3
4. Tip 4
5. Tip 5

Chapter 2: Home and Garden Hacks
1. Tip 1
2. Tip 2
3. Tip 3
4. Tip 4
5. Tip 5

Chapter 3: Kitchen and Cooking Tips
1. Tip 1
2. Tip 2
3. Tip 3
4. Tip 4
5. Tip 5

Chapter 4: Smart Shopping and Resource Management
1. Tip 1
2. Tip 2
3. Tip 3
4. Tip 4

5. Tip 5

Chapter 5: Eco-Friendly Practices

1. Tip 1
2. Tip 2
3. Tip 3
4. Tip 4
5. Tip 5

Conclusion

- Recap of Key Points
- Encouragement to Continue Adopting Frugal and Productive Habits
- Invitation for Reader Feedback

Appendix

- Additional Resources
    - Books, Websites, and Tools for Further Reading and Exploration
- Worksheets and Templates
    - Budget Templates, DIY Project Plans, and Frugality Trackers

Introduction

Revisiting the Importance of Frugal Living

In the first volume, we explored the foundational principles of frugal living, focusing on how small, mindful changes can significantly impact your financial stability and overall well-being. As we continue this journey in Volume 2, we will delve deeper into creative, practical, and sustainable tips that will further enhance your frugal lifestyle. Frugal living is not about deprivation but about making smarter choices that lead to a more fulfilling and resource-efficient life.

Expanding Your Frugal and Productive Habits

This volume introduces 25 new tips that cover a wide range of areas, from DIY projects and home management to eco-friendly practices and smart shopping strategies. Each tip is designed to be easily implementable, with detailed instructions, real-life examples, and practical advice to integrate these habits into your daily routine. By embracing these tips, you will continue to save money, reduce waste, and increase your productivity, all while enjoying a richer and more sustainable lifestyle.

What You'll Learn in This Volume

In Volume 2, you will learn how to create DIY home decor, repurpose household items, improve your cooking and gardening skills, manage resources more efficiently, and adopt eco-friendly practices. Each chapter focuses on a specific aspect of frugal living, providing you with a comprehensive guide to enhancing your frugality and productivity. Let's dive into the first chapter and start exploring these valuable tips.

Chapter 1: Creative DIY Projects

Tip 1: Create DIY Home Decor

Introduction

Why This Tip Matters: Creating your own home decor is a cost-effective way to personalize your living space. It allows you to express your creativity, reduce waste, and avoid the high costs of store-bought decorations.

In-Depth Information

How to Create DIY Home Decor:

1. **Materials Needed:**
   - Recycled materials (e.g., old jars, pallets, fabric scraps)
   - Craft supplies (paint, glue, scissors)
   - Decorative items (ribbons, beads, buttons)
2. **Steps:**
   - Identify areas in your home that could benefit from new decor.
   - Gather recycled materials and craft supplies.
   - Use online tutorials or your creativity to design and create unique decor items.
   - Examples include painted mason jars, pallet wood wall art, and fabric bunting.

Real-Life Example

Example: Emma transformed her living room by creating a gallery wall using old frames she painted and filled with family photos and handmade art. She enjoyed the creative process and saved money while making her home feel more personalized.

Implementation in Daily Life

How to Incorporate DIY Home Decor:

- **For Special Occasions:** Create seasonal decor items to celebrate holidays and events.
- **For Gifts:** Make personalized decor items as thoughtful, handmade gifts for friends and family.
- **For Continuous Improvement:** Regularly update and rotate your DIY decor to keep your home feeling fresh and new.

Maintenance Tips:

- Use high-quality materials to ensure durability.
- Clean and maintain decor items regularly to keep them looking their best.
- Store seasonal decor items safely to use year after year.

Tip 2: Repurpose Old Blankets into Pet Beds

Introduction

Why This Tip Matters: Repurposing old blankets into pet beds is an excellent way to recycle materials while providing comfort for your pets. This tip helps reduce waste and saves money on buying new pet supplies.

In-Depth Information

How to Repurpose Old Blankets into Pet Beds:

1. **Materials Needed:**

- Old blankets
- Scissors
- Needle and thread or sewing machine
- Stuffing (optional, for added comfort)

2. **Steps:**
   - Cut the blankets into desired sizes for the pet beds.
   - Fold and sew the edges to create a durable cover.
   - Add stuffing if needed, and sew the opening closed.
   - You can also create removable covers for easy washing.

Real-Life Example

Example: John repurposed an old fleece blanket into a cozy bed for his dog, Max. He enjoyed the project and Max loved his new bed, making it a win-win situation.

Implementation in Daily Life

How to Use Repurposed Pet Beds:

- **For Comfort:** Place the beds in your pet's favorite spots around the house.
- **For Travel:** Use these beds in pet carriers or cars for added comfort during travel.
- **For Multiple Pets:** Make multiple beds to ensure all your pets have a cozy place to rest.

Maintenance Tips:

- Wash the pet beds regularly to keep them clean and hygienic.
- Repair any tears or damage promptly to extend the life of the beds.

- Rotate the beds occasionally to even out wear and tear.

Tip 3: Refinish Old Furniture

Introduction

Why This Tip Matters: Refinishing old furniture is a cost-effective way to update your home decor without buying new pieces. It also promotes sustainability by giving new life to items that might otherwise be discarded.

In-Depth Information

How to Refinish Old Furniture:

1. **Materials Needed:**
   - Sandpaper or electric sander
   - Paint or wood stain
   - Brushes and rollers
   - Sealant or varnish
2. **Steps:**
   - Choose a piece of furniture that needs refinishing.
   - Sand the surface to remove old paint or finish and smooth out imperfections.
   - Apply a coat of primer if painting, or a pre-stain conditioner if staining.
   - Paint or stain the furniture with your chosen color or finish.
   - Apply a sealant or varnish to protect the surface and enhance durability.

Real-Life Example

Example: Sarah refinished an old wooden dresser she found at a garage sale. After sanding and painting it with a modern color, it became a beautiful and functional piece in her bedroom.

Implementation in Daily Life
How to Refinish Furniture:

- **For Home Decor:** Update your furniture to match your current decor style.
- **For Gifts:** Refinish furniture pieces as unique, personalized gifts for friends and family.
- **For Sustainability:** Regularly maintain and refinish furniture to extend its life and reduce waste.

Maintenance Tips:

- Clean and dust refinished furniture regularly to preserve the finish.
- Use coasters and placemats to protect surfaces from damage.
- Touch up any scratches or chips promptly to maintain the appearance.

Tip 4: Recycle Old Candles into New Ones
Introduction

Why This Tip Matters: Recycling old candles into new ones is a frugal and sustainable way to enjoy your favorite scents without buying new candles. This tip helps reduce waste and makes the most of leftover candle wax.

In-Depth Information
How to Recycle Old Candles:

1. **Materials Needed:**
    - Old candle wax
    - New wicks
    - Candle molds or containers

- Double boiler or microwave-safe container

2. **Steps:**
    - Collect and clean the leftover wax from old candles.
    - Melt the wax using a double boiler or microwave in short intervals.
    - Place a new wick in the center of your mold or container.
    - Pour the melted wax into the mold, holding the wick upright.
    - Allow the wax to cool and harden completely before trimming the wick.

Real-Life Example

Example: Lisa gathered all her old candle remnants and melted them down to create new layered candles. She enjoyed the process and loved the unique, multicolored results.

Implementation in Daily Life

How to Use Recycled Candles:

- **For Home Use:** Place the new candles around your home for ambiance and fragrance.
- **For Gifts:** Package the candles in decorative jars and give them as thoughtful, handmade gifts.
- **For Crafting:** Experiment with different molds and scents to create customized candles.

Maintenance Tips:

- Store leftover wax in a cool, dry place for future use.
- Use heat-safe containers to avoid cracks or breaks.

- Trim wicks to ¼ inch before each use to ensure even burning.

Tip 5: Make Your Own Furniture Polish

Introduction

Why This Tip Matters: Making your own furniture polish is a natural and cost-effective way to keep your wooden furniture looking its best. Homemade polish is free from harmful chemicals and can be made with common household ingredients.

In-Depth Information

How to Make Furniture Polish:

1. **Ingredients Needed:**
    - Olive oil or vegetable oil
    - White vinegar or lemon juice
    - Essential oils (optional, for fragrance)
2. **Steps:**
    - Mix 2 parts oil with 1 part vinegar or lemon juice in a spray bottle.
    - Add a few drops of essential oil if desired.
    - Shake well before each use.
    - Apply a small amount to a soft cloth and rub onto the furniture in circular motions.
    - Buff with a clean cloth for a shiny finish.

Real-Life Example

Example: Tom started making his own furniture polish using olive oil and lemon juice. He found it worked just as well as store-bought polish, and he appreciated the natural ingredients.

Implementation in Daily Life

How to Use Homemade Furniture Polish:

- **For Regular Cleaning:** Use the polish regularly to maintain the shine and condition of wooden furniture.
- **For Deep Cleaning:** Apply a generous amount and let it sit for a few minutes before buffing to remove built-up grime.
- **For Fragrance:** Add essential oils for a pleasant scent while cleaning.

Maintenance Tips:

- Store the polish in a cool, dark place.
- Shake the bottle well before each use to mix the ingredients.
- Test the polish on a small, inconspicuous area before applying to the entire surface.

Chapter 2: Home and Garden Hacks

Tip 1: Store Vegetables in a Sandbox to Keep Them Fresh

Introduction

Why This Tip Matters: Storing vegetables in a sandbox is an old-fashioned method that helps keep root vegetables fresh for extended periods. This technique can save you money by reducing food waste and allowing you to buy vegetables in bulk when they are in season.

In-Depth Information

How to Store Vegetables in a Sandbox:

1. **Materials Needed:**
    - Clean, dry sandbox or wooden box
    - Sand (preferably clean, coarse sand)
    - Root vegetables (carrots, beets, turnips, etc.)
2. **Steps:**
    - Clean the vegetables thoroughly and let them dry completely.
    - Fill the sandbox with a layer of sand.
    - Place the vegetables in the sand, making sure they do not touch each other.
    - Cover the vegetables with more sand.
    - Store the sandbox in a cool, dark place like a basement or garage.

Real-Life Example

Example: Julia used this method to store her fall harvest of carrots and beets. She found that the vegetables stayed fresh and crisp for several months, which allowed her to enjoy garden-fresh produce all winter long.

Implementation in Daily Life

How to Use Stored Vegetables:

- **For Cooking:** Use the stored vegetables in soups, stews, and salads throughout the winter.
- **For Snacking:** Enjoy fresh, crunchy vegetables as healthy snacks.
- **For Preserving:** Extend the storage life by canning or pickling surplus vegetables.

Maintenance Tips:

- Check the sand and vegetables periodically for moisture and rot.
- Replace the sand if it becomes damp or contaminated.
- Rotate the vegetables to ensure they all stay fresh.

Tip 2: Save Seeds from Your Garden for Next Season

Introduction

Why This Tip Matters: Saving seeds from your garden allows you to grow your favorite plants year after year without buying new seeds. This practice is economical, sustainable, and helps preserve heirloom varieties.

In-Depth Information
How to Save Seeds:

1. **Materials Needed:**
   - Mature plants with seeds
   - Paper bags or envelopes
   - Labels
2. **Steps:**
   - Allow plants to mature and go to seed.
   - Collect seeds from the plants, ensuring they are fully ripe.
   - Dry the seeds thoroughly in a cool, dry place.
   - Store seeds in labeled paper bags or envelopes.
   - Keep the seeds in a cool, dark place until planting season.

Real-Life Example

Example: Ben saved seeds from his heirloom tomato plants and used them to grow new plants the following year. He found that the saved seeds produced robust, healthy plants that yielded a bountiful harvest.

Implementation in Daily Life
How to Use Saved Seeds:

- **For Planting:** Use the saved seeds to start your garden in the next season.
- **For Sharing:** Share seeds with friends and neighbors to promote gardening and sustainability.
- **For Preserving Varieties:** Maintain the genetic diversity of heirloom and rare plant varieties.

Maintenance Tips:

- Ensure seeds are completely dry before storing to prevent mold.
- Label seeds with the plant name and collection date for easy identification.
- Test seed viability by germinating a few seeds before planting season.

Tip 3: Line Dry Clothes Outdoors

Introduction

Why This Tip Matters: Line drying clothes outdoors is an energy-efficient way to dry laundry. It saves money on electricity bills, extends the life of your clothes, and adds a fresh, natural scent.

In-Depth Information

How to Line Dry Clothes:

1. **Materials Needed:**
    - Clothesline or drying rack
    - Clothespins
2. **Steps:**
    - Set up a clothesline in a sunny, breezy area of your yard or balcony.
    - Hang wet clothes on the line using clothespins, spacing them out for optimal airflow.
    - Allow clothes to dry completely before removing.

Real-Life Example

Example: Laura started line drying her clothes in the backyard and noticed a significant reduction in her electricity bill. She also appreciated how the sun naturally whitened her whites and left all her clothes smelling fresh.

Implementation in Daily Life

How to Line Dry Clothes:

- **For Everyday Use:** Make line drying a regular part of your laundry routine.
- **For Special Items:** Use line drying for delicate items that can't go in the dryer.
- **For Large Loads:** Utilize multiple lines or a drying rack to accommodate bigger loads.

Maintenance Tips:

- Clean the clothesline regularly to prevent dirt and stains on clothes.
- Bring clothes inside promptly to avoid exposure to dew or rain.
- Use sturdy clothespins to keep clothes securely fastened to the line.

Tip 4: Create a Compost Heap for Garden Fertilizer

Introduction

Why This Tip Matters: Creating a compost heap is a fantastic way to recycle kitchen and garden waste into nutrient-rich fertilizer for your plants. It reduces landfill waste and provides an organic, cost-free way to enhance soil health.

In-Depth Information

How to Create a Compost Heap:

1. **Materials Needed:**
    - Compost bin or designated area in your yard
    - Kitchen scraps (vegetable peels, coffee grounds, eggshells)
    - Yard waste (leaves, grass clippings, small branches)
2. **Steps:**
    - Choose a spot for your compost heap or set up a compost bin.
    - Add kitchen scraps and yard waste, ensuring a balance of green (nitrogen-rich) and brown (carbon-rich) materials.
    - Turn the compost regularly to aerate and speed up decomposition.
    - Monitor moisture levels and add water if the compost becomes too dry.

Real-Life Example

Example: Kevin set up a compost heap in his backyard and started composting his kitchen scraps and yard waste. Within a few months, he had rich, dark compost to use in his vegetable garden, leading to healthier plants and bigger yields.

Implementation in Daily Life

How to Use Compost:

- **For Gardening:** Mix compost into the soil to improve fertility and structure.
- **For Potting Soil:** Use compost as a component of homemade potting mixes.
- **For Lawn Care:** Top-dress your lawn with compost to promote healthy grass growth.

Maintenance Tips:

- Avoid adding meat, dairy, and oily foods to the compost to prevent odors and pests.
- Chop large items into smaller pieces to speed up decomposition.
- Keep the compost heap covered to retain moisture and heat.

Tip 5: Repair Leaky Faucets to Save Water

Introduction

Why This Tip Matters: Repairing leaky faucets is a simple yet effective way to conserve water and reduce your utility bills. Even small leaks can waste significant amounts of water over time, so prompt repairs are essential.

In-Depth Information
How to Repair Leaky Faucets:

1. **Materials Needed:**
   - Replacement parts (washers, O-rings, cartridges)
   - Screwdriver
   - Wrench
   - Plumber's tape
2. **Steps:**
   - Turn off the water supply to the faucet.
   - Disassemble the faucet to identify the source of the leak.
   - Replace worn or damaged parts with new ones.
   - Reassemble the faucet and turn the water supply back on.
   - Check for leaks and make any necessary adjustments.

Real-Life Example

Example: Jane fixed a leaky kitchen faucet with a simple washer replacement. The repair took just a few minutes and saved her from wasting gallons of water each month.

Implementation in Daily Life
How to Maintain Faucets:

- **For Regular Maintenance:** Check faucets periodically for signs of leaks and wear.
- **For Immediate Action:** Repair leaks as soon as they are detected to prevent water waste.

- **For Professional Help:** Consult a plumber if you encounter complex issues beyond your skill level.

Maintenance Tips:

- Keep spare washers and O-rings on hand for quick repairs.
- Clean faucet aerators regularly to maintain water flow.
- Apply plumber's tape to threaded connections to prevent leaks.

Chapter 3: Kitchen and Cooking Tips

Tip 1: Use a Solar Oven for Cooking

Introduction

Why This Tip Matters: Using a solar oven for cooking harnesses the power of the sun to prepare meals, reducing your reliance on conventional energy sources. It's an eco-friendly, cost-effective way to cook, especially during sunny days.

In-Depth Information

How to Use a Solar Oven:

1. **Materials Needed:**
    - Solar oven (purchased or homemade)
    - Cookware (dark-colored pots and pans)
2. **Steps:**
    - Position the solar oven in a sunny spot, ensuring it's angled to capture maximum sunlight.
    - Preheat the oven for about 30 minutes.
    - Place your food in dark-colored cookware to absorb heat efficiently.
    - Put the cookware in the solar oven and close the lid.
    - Monitor the cooking process and adjust the oven's position as needed to follow the sun.

Real-Life Example

Example: Mark built a simple solar oven using cardboard and aluminum foil. He enjoyed cooking meals outdoors, especially during summer, and appreciated the energy savings.

Implementation in Daily Life

How to Use a Solar Oven:

- **For Baking:** Bake bread, cookies, and casseroles using solar energy.
- **For Slow Cooking:** Prepare stews, soups, and other slow-cooked dishes.
- **For Outdoor Cooking:** Use the solar oven for picnics and camping trips.

Maintenance Tips:

- Clean the oven regularly to ensure maximum efficiency.
- Store the oven indoors when not in use to protect it from the elements.
- Replace reflective materials if they become damaged or dull.

Tip 2: Make Homemade Pasta

Introduction

Why This Tip Matters: Making homemade pasta is a rewarding way to enjoy fresh, delicious pasta without the additives and preservatives found in store-bought versions. It's also cost-effective and allows you to customize the pasta to your liking.

In-Depth Information

How to Make Homemade Pasta:

1. **Ingredients Needed:**
   - Flour
   - Eggs
   - Salt
   - Water (if needed)
2. **Steps:**
   - Combine 2 cups of flour and a pinch of salt on a clean surface.
   - Make a well in the center and crack 2 eggs into it.
   - Gradually mix the eggs and flour, kneading until a dough forms.
   - If the dough is too dry, add a small amount of water.
   - Knead the dough for about 10 minutes until smooth and elastic.
   - Cover the dough and let it rest for 30 minutes.
   - Roll out the dough and cut into desired shapes.
   - Cook the pasta in boiling salted water until al dente.

Real-Life Example

Example: Maria started making homemade pasta as a fun weekend project. She loved experimenting with different shapes and flavors, and her family enjoyed the fresh, homemade taste.

Implementation in Daily Life

How to Use Homemade Pasta:

- **For Family Meals:** Prepare fresh pasta for special family dinners.

- **For Entertaining:** Impress guests with homemade pasta dishes.
- **For Customization:** Add herbs or spices to the dough for unique flavors.

Maintenance Tips:

- Store unused dough in the refrigerator for up to 2 days.
- Dry extra pasta thoroughly and store in an airtight container.
- Clean pasta-making equipment promptly to prevent dough from hardening.

Tip 3: Make Your Own Mustard and Ketchup

Introduction

Why This Tip Matters: Making your own mustard and ketchup is a simple way to avoid the additives and preservatives found in store-bought condiments. Homemade versions can be tailored to your taste preferences and are often more cost-effective.

In-Depth Information

How to Make Mustard:

1. **Ingredients Needed:**
    - Mustard seeds
    - Vinegar
    - Water
    - Salt
    - Honey (optional)
2. **Steps:**

- Soak ½ cup of mustard seeds in ½ cup of vinegar and ½ cup of water for 24-48 hours.
- Blend the soaked seeds with 1 teaspoon of salt and honey to taste.
- Adjust the consistency with more water if needed.
- Store in a glass jar and refrigerate.

How to Make Ketchup:

1. **Ingredients Needed:**
    - Tomato paste
    - Vinegar
    - Brown sugar
    - Salt
    - Spices (garlic powder, onion powder, paprika)
2. **Steps:**
    - Combine a 6-ounce can of tomato paste with ¼ cup of vinegar, ¼ cup of brown sugar, 1 teaspoon of salt, and spices to taste.
    - Mix until smooth.
    - Adjust sweetness and seasoning as desired.
    - Store in a glass jar and refrigerate.

Real-Life Example

Example: Sarah started making her own mustard and ketchup to control the ingredients and flavors. She enjoyed the process and loved the fresh, homemade taste of her condiments.

Implementation in Daily Life

How to Use Homemade Mustard and Ketchup:

- **For Meals:** Use as condiments for sandwiches, burgers, and hot dogs.
- **For Cooking:** Incorporate into recipes for added flavor.
- **For Gifting:** Package in decorative jars and give as gifts.

Maintenance Tips:

- Store homemade condiments in the refrigerator to maintain freshness.
- Use clean utensils to avoid contamination.
- Label jars with the date to track freshness.

Tip 4: Bake Granola Bars with Nuts and Honey

Introduction

Why This Tip Matters: Baking your own granola bars is a healthy and cost-effective alternative to store-bought versions. You can control the ingredients, avoid preservatives, and customize the bars to your taste.

In-Depth Information

How to Bake Granola Bars:

1. **Ingredients Needed:**
    - Rolled oats
    - Nuts and seeds
    - Dried fruit
    - Honey or maple syrup
    - Nut butter
2. **Steps:**

- Preheat the oven to 350°F (175°C).
- Mix 2 cups of rolled oats, 1 cup of nuts and seeds, and 1 cup of dried fruit in a large bowl.
- In a separate bowl, combine ½ cup of honey or maple syrup with ½ cup of nut butter.
- Pour the wet ingredients into the dry ingredients and mix well.
- Press the mixture into a lined baking pan.
- Bake for 20-25 minutes until golden brown.
- Let cool completely before cutting into bars.

Real-Life Example

Example: Tom started making granola bars to have healthy snacks for his busy workdays. He enjoyed experimenting with different ingredients and found that the homemade bars were a tasty, nutritious option.

Implementation in Daily Life

How to Use Homemade Granola Bars:

- **For Snacks:** Pack in lunchboxes or take on-the-go for a quick snack.
- **For Breakfast:** Enjoy as a convenient breakfast option.
- **For Gifting:** Wrap in decorative packaging and give as homemade gifts.

Maintenance Tips:

- Store granola bars in an airtight container to maintain freshness.

- Experiment with different ingredient combinations for variety.
- Label the bars with the date to track freshness.

Tip 5: Make Your Own Bread to Save Money

Introduction

Why This Tip Matters: Making your own bread is a cost-effective way to enjoy fresh, delicious bread without the additives and preservatives found in store-bought versions. It's also a rewarding and satisfying baking project.

In-Depth Information

How to Make Bread:

1. **Ingredients Needed:**
    - Flour
    - Yeast
    - Water
    - Salt
    - Sugar or honey (optional)
2. **Steps:**
    - Combine 3 cups of flour, 1 teaspoon of salt, and 1 tablespoon of sugar or honey in a large bowl.
    - Dissolve 1 packet of yeast in 1 cup of warm water and let it sit for 5 minutes.
    - Add the yeast mixture to the dry ingredients and mix until a dough forms.
    - Knead the dough on a floured surface for about 10 minutes until smooth and elastic.

- Place the dough in a greased bowl, cover, and let it rise in a warm place for about 1 hour.
- Punch down the dough, shape it into a loaf, and place it in a greased loaf pan.
- Let it rise again for 30-45 minutes.
- Preheat the oven to 375°F (190°C) and bake the bread for 30-35 minutes until golden brown.
- Let the bread cool before slicing.

Real-Life Example

Example: Emily started baking her own bread as a weekend project. She loved the fresh, homemade taste and found that it was much cheaper than buying artisanal bread from the store.

Implementation in Daily Life

How to Use Homemade Bread:

- **For Meals:** Enjoy fresh bread with meals or as a base for sandwiches.
- **For Baking Projects:** Experiment with different types of bread, such as whole wheat, sourdough, and flavored loaves.
- **For Gifting:** Share homemade bread with friends and family as a thoughtful, delicious gift.

Maintenance Tips:

- Store bread in a cool, dry place to maintain freshness.
- Use airtight containers or bread bags to prevent staleness.
- Freeze extra loaves to extend shelf life.

Chapter 4: Smart Shopping and Resource Management

Tip 1: Use a Thermos for Keeping Drinks Hot or Cold

Introduction

Why This Tip Matters: Using a thermos for keeping drinks hot or cold is a practical way to maintain the temperature of your beverages throughout the day. It's cost-effective, reduces waste from disposable cups, and ensures you always have your favorite drink at the perfect temperature.

In-Depth Information

How to Use a Thermos:

1. **Choosing a Thermos:**
   - Look for a thermos with good insulation properties.
   - Consider size and capacity based on your needs.
2. **Steps:**
   - Preheat or pre-cool the thermos by filling it with hot or cold water for a few minutes.
   - Empty the water and fill the thermos with your desired beverage.
   - Seal the thermos tightly to maintain the temperature.

Real-Life Example

Example: David started using a thermos to keep his coffee hot during his morning commute. He enjoyed having his favorite brew at the perfect temperature and appreciated not having to buy coffee in disposable cups.

Implementation in Daily Life

How to Use a Thermos:

- **For Work:** Bring hot coffee, tea, or soup to work in a thermos.
- **For Travel:** Use a thermos to keep drinks at the right temperature during trips.
- **For Outdoor Activities:** Take hot or cold beverages on hikes, picnics, or sporting events.

Maintenance Tips:

- Clean the thermos thoroughly after each use to prevent odors and residue.
- Use a bottle brush to reach and clean all areas.
- Store the thermos with the lid off to allow it to air out.

Tip 2: Save Buttons from Old Clothes

Introduction

Why This Tip Matters: Saving buttons from old clothes is a simple way to have a ready supply of replacement buttons for future sewing projects. It's a cost-effective practice that also helps reduce waste.

In-Depth Information

How to Save Buttons:

1. **Materials Needed:**
   - Old clothes with buttons
   - Scissors or seam ripper
   - Small container or jar
2. **Steps:**
   - Carefully cut or rip the buttons off old clothes using scissors or a seam ripper.
   - Clean the buttons if necessary.
   - Store the buttons in a small container or jar.

Real-Life Example

Example: Emma collected buttons from old, worn-out clothes and stored them in a decorative jar. She found it convenient to have a variety of buttons on hand for sewing projects and repairs.

Implementation in Daily Life

How to Use Saved Buttons:

- **For Repairs:** Replace lost or broken buttons on clothes, bags, and other items.
- **For Craft Projects:** Use buttons in DIY crafts, such as button art, jewelry, and decorations.
- **For Customization:** Add unique buttons to new sewing projects for a personalized touch.

Maintenance Tips:

- Sort buttons by size and color for easy access.
- Keep buttons in a dry, secure container to prevent loss and damage.
- Regularly check your button collection and discard any damaged or unusable buttons.

Tip 3: Make a Grocery List to Avoid Impulse Buying

Introduction

Why This Tip Matters: Making a grocery list before shopping helps you stay focused, avoid impulse buys, and save money. It ensures you buy only what you need and reduces the risk of food waste.

In-Depth Information

How to Make a Grocery List:

1. **Materials Needed:**
   - Pen and paper or a grocery list app
2. **Steps:**
   - Plan your meals for the week to determine what you need to buy.
   - Check your pantry and fridge to see what items you already have.
   - Write down the items you need, categorized by section of the store (e.g., produce, dairy, meats).
   - Stick to the list while shopping to avoid unnecessary purchases.

Real-Life Example

Example: Sarah started making detailed grocery lists before shopping. She noticed she spent less money and had fewer food items going to waste. The practice also made her shopping trips quicker and more efficient.

Implementation in Daily Life

How to Use a Grocery List:

- **For Meal Planning:** Base your list on planned meals to ensure you have all necessary ingredients.
- **For Budgeting:** Use the list to keep track of your spending and avoid overspending.
- **For Reducing Waste:** Buy only what you need to minimize food waste.

Maintenance Tips:

- Keep a notepad or app handy to add items to the list as you run out.
- Review and update your list regularly to reflect your changing needs.
- Stick to the list as closely as possible to avoid impulse purchases.

Tip 4: Sew Reusable Shopping Bags from Old Fabric

Introduction

Why This Tip Matters: Sewing reusable shopping bags from old fabric is an eco-friendly and cost-effective alternative to using disposable plastic bags. It helps reduce plastic waste and allows you to recycle old materials into something useful.

In-Depth Information

How to Sew Reusable Shopping Bags:

1. **Materials Needed:**
   - Old fabric (e.g., old clothes, sheets, or curtains)
   - Scissors
   - Sewing machine or needle and thread
2. **Steps:**

- Cut the fabric into two equal rectangles.
- Place the rectangles right sides together and sew along three sides, leaving one side open.
- Turn the bag right side out.
- Fold and sew a hem on the open side to create a finished edge.
- Cut and sew two long strips of fabric for handles.
- Attach the handles to the bag.

Real-Life Example

Example: Lisa made several reusable shopping bags from old curtains. She enjoyed the creative process and appreciated having sturdy, eco-friendly bags for her grocery trips.

Implementation in Daily Life

How to Use Reusable Shopping Bags:

- **For Groceries:** Use the bags for grocery shopping to reduce plastic waste.
- **For Errands:** Carry the bags with you for other shopping trips and errands.
- **For Gifting:** Make and give reusable bags as practical, eco-friendly gifts.

Maintenance Tips:

- Wash the bags regularly to keep them clean and hygienic.
- Repair any tears or damage to extend their lifespan.
- Store the bags in an easily accessible place to remember to use them.

Tip 5: Find Treasures and Necessities at Garage and Estate Sales

Introduction

Why This Tip Matters: Shopping at garage and estate sales is a great way to find unique items and necessities at a fraction of the retail price. It's an eco-friendly practice that promotes recycling and reduces the demand for new goods.

In-Depth Information

How to Shop at Garage and Estate Sales:

1. **Tips for Finding Sales:**
   - Check local listings, newspapers, and online platforms for sale announcements.
   - Plan your route to visit multiple sales in one trip.
2. **Steps:**
   - Arrive early to get the best selection.
   - Bring cash in small denominations for easier transactions.
   - Be prepared to negotiate prices.
   - Inspect items carefully for quality and condition before purchasing.

Real-Life Example

Example: Tom found several valuable items, including vintage furniture and kitchenware, at estate sales. He enjoyed the thrill of the hunt and the satisfaction of finding high-quality items at low prices.

Implementation in Daily Life

How to Use Garage and Estate Sale Finds:

- **For Home Decor:** Find unique, affordable items to decorate your home.
- **For Gifting:** Purchase high-quality items as thoughtful, budget-friendly gifts.
- **For Resale:** Buy valuable items to resell for a profit.

Maintenance Tips:

- Clean and sanitize items before using them.
- Research the value of potential purchases to avoid overpaying.
- Regularly check local listings to stay updated on upcoming sales.

Chapter 5: Eco-Friendly Practices

Tip 1: Use Homemade Insect Repellent

Introduction

Why This Tip Matters: Using homemade insect repellent is a natural and cost-effective way to protect yourself from insects without the harmful chemicals found in commercial products. It's safe for both your family and the environment.

In-Depth Information

How to Make Homemade Insect Repellent:

1. **Ingredients Needed:**
    - Essential oils (e.g., citronella, eucalyptus, lavender)
    - Witch hazel or vodka
    - Water
    - Spray bottle
2. **Steps:**
    - Combine 10-20 drops of essential oils with 2 tablespoons of witch hazel or vodka.
    - Add 2 ounces of water and mix well.
    - Pour the mixture into a spray bottle.
    - Shake well before each use and spray on exposed skin.

Real-Life Example

Example: Kevin started making his own insect repellent using essential oils. He found it effective and appreciated the natural ingredients, especially when using it on his children.

Implementation in Daily Life

How to Use Homemade Insect Repellent:

- **For Outdoor Activities:** Apply before hiking, camping, or gardening.
- **For Home Use:** Spray around windows and doors to keep insects out.
- **For Pets:** Use a diluted version to protect pets from insects.

Maintenance Tips:

- Store the repellent in a cool, dark place to maintain potency.
- Shake well before each use to mix the ingredients.
- Reapply as needed, especially after sweating or swimming.

Tip 2: Use a Hand Whisk Instead of an Electric Mixer

Introduction

Why This Tip Matters: Using a hand whisk instead of an electric mixer saves energy and gives you better control over mixing. It's a simple switch that can make a difference in your energy consumption and the quality of your cooking.

In-Depth Information

How to Use a Hand Whisk:

1. **Choosing a Hand Whisk:**
   - Look for a sturdy, well-made whisk.

- Consider different sizes for various tasks.
2. **Steps:**
    - Use the whisk to mix ingredients in a circular motion.
    - Adjust the speed and pressure based on the task (e.g., slow for gentle mixing, fast for whipping).
    - Clean the whisk promptly after use to prevent residue build-up.

Real-Life Example

Example: Jane switched to using a hand whisk for most of her baking and cooking tasks. She enjoyed the control it gave her over the mixing process and appreciated the energy savings.

Implementation in Daily Life

How to Use a Hand Whisk:

- **For Baking:** Use for mixing batters, whipping cream, and beating eggs.
- **For Cooking:** Use for stirring sauces, dressings, and other mixtures.
- **For Everyday Tasks:** Use for simple kitchen tasks to save energy and improve results.

Maintenance Tips:

- Wash the whisk immediately after use to prevent food from hardening.
- Store the whisk in a dry place to prevent rust.
- Check for and replace any worn or damaged parts.

Tip 3: Use a Hand Crank Coffee Grinder

Introduction

Why This Tip Matters: Using a hand crank coffee grinder is a manual, energy-saving alternative to electric grinders. It provides a consistent grind, enhances the flavor of your coffee, and reduces your carbon footprint.

In-Depth Information

How to Use a Hand Crank Coffee Grinder:

1. **Choosing a Hand Crank Grinder:**
   - Look for a durable grinder with adjustable settings.
   - Consider the size and capacity based on your needs.
2. **Steps:**
   - Fill the grinder with coffee beans.
   - Adjust the grind setting based on your brewing method (e.g., coarse for French press, fine for espresso).
   - Turn the crank handle to grind the beans.
   - Collect the ground coffee and use as desired.

Real-Life Example

Example: Alex switched to a hand crank coffee grinder for his morning coffee ritual. He enjoyed the manual process and found that the freshly ground coffee had a richer, more robust flavor.

Implementation in Daily Life

How to Use a Hand Crank Coffee Grinder:

- **For Daily Brewing:** Grind fresh coffee beans each morning for the best flavor.
- **For Travel:** Use a portable hand grinder for fresh coffee on the go.
- **For Different Methods:** Adjust the grind size for various brewing methods.

Maintenance Tips:

- Clean the grinder regularly to prevent build-up of coffee oils.
- Store in a dry place to avoid rust.
- Check and replace any worn parts as needed.

Tip 4: Use Homemade Potpourri for Natural Air Freshening

Introduction

Why This Tip Matters: Using homemade potpourri is a natural and cost-effective way to freshen the air in your home without chemical air fresheners. It's customizable and can be made from dried flowers, herbs, and spices you already have.

In-Depth Information

How to Make Homemade Potpourri:

1. **Ingredients Needed:**
   - Dried flowers (e.g., roses, lavender)
   - Dried herbs (e.g., rosemary, thyme)
   - Spices (e.g., cinnamon sticks, cloves)
   - Essential oils (optional)
2. **Steps:**
   - Combine dried flowers, herbs, and spices in a bowl.

- Add a few drops of essential oil for extra fragrance.
- Mix well and place the potpourri in a decorative bowl or sachet.
- Refresh the potpourri with more essential oil as needed.

Real-Life Example

Example: Emily made a batch of homemade potpourri using dried roses and lavender from her garden. She enjoyed the natural fragrance and appreciated avoiding commercial air fresheners.

Implementation in Daily Life

How to Use Homemade Potpourri:

- **For Home:** Place bowls of potpourri in different rooms for continuous fragrance.
- **For Gifts:** Package potpourri in decorative sachets and give as gifts.
- **For Seasonal Decor:** Make themed potpourri for different seasons and holidays.

Maintenance Tips:

- Store dried ingredients in a cool, dark place to maintain their fragrance.
- Refresh potpourri with essential oils to prolong the scent.
- Discard and replace potpourri when it loses its fragrance.

Tip 5: Use Cornstarch Paste for Streak-Free Window Cleaning

Introduction

Why This Tip Matters: Using cornstarch paste for window cleaning is a natural and effective way to achieve streak-free windows without commercial cleaners. It's eco-friendly and uses simple ingredients you likely already have.

In-Depth Information

How to Make Cornstarch Paste:

1. **Ingredients Needed:**
    - Cornstarch
    - Water
    - Vinegar
    - Spray bottle
    - Clean cloth or squeegee
2. **Steps:**
    - Mix 1 tablespoon of cornstarch with 1 cup of water and 1 cup of vinegar.
    - Pour the mixture into a spray bottle.
    - Shake well before each use.
    - Spray the solution onto windows and wipe with a clean cloth or squeegee for a streak-free finish.

Real-Life Example

Example: Lisa started using cornstarch paste to clean her windows and mirrors. She found it worked better than commercial cleaners and appreciated the natural ingredients.

Implementation in Daily Life

How to Use Cornstarch Paste:

- **For Windows:** Use regularly to keep windows clean and streak-free.
- **For Mirrors:** Clean mirrors for a clear, streak-free shine.
- **For Glass Surfaces:** Use on glass tabletops and other glass surfaces.

Maintenance Tips:

- Shake the solution well before each use to mix the cornstarch.
- Store the spray bottle in a cool, dark place.
- Use a clean cloth or squeegee to avoid leaving streaks.

Conclusion

Recap of Key Points

In this second volume, we have delved deeper into the world of frugal living and productivity, exploring another 25 tips that span various aspects of home and garden hacks, kitchen and cooking tips, smart shopping and resource management, and eco-friendly practices. Each tip provided you with detailed instructions, real-life examples, and practical advice to incorporate these habits into your daily routine. By adopting these strategies, you continue to save money, reduce waste, and enhance your overall well-being.

Encouragement to Continue Adopting Frugal and Productive Habits

As you move forward, remember that frugal living is a journey, not a destination. The more you practice these tips, the more natural they will become. Every small change adds up to significant savings and a more sustainable lifestyle. Keep experimenting, stay creative, and share your successes with others. Your efforts contribute not only to your personal financial health but also to the well-being of our planet.

Invitation for Reader Feedback

We value your feedback and experiences. Have you tried any of the tips in this volume? Did you find them helpful? Are there other areas you'd like us to cover in future books? Your input helps us improve and tailor our content to better meet your needs. Please share your thoughts and suggestions with us via email or through our website. We look forward to hearing from you and continuing this journey together.

Appendix
Additional Resources
Books:

- "DIY Projects for the Self-Sufficient Homeowner" by Betsy Matheson: A comprehensive guide to home improvement and self-sufficiency.
- "The Urban Homestead" by Kelly Coyne and Erik Knutzen: Ideas for city dwellers to live sustainably and frugally.
- "The Frugal Gardener" by Catriona Tudor Erler: Tips and techniques for maintaining a beautiful garden on a budget.

Websites:

- **Instructables:** instructables.com: A community of DIY enthusiasts sharing step-by-step projects and ideas.
- **ThriftyFun:** thriftyfun.com: A resource for frugal living tips, recipes, and DIY projects.
- **The Prairie Homestead:** theprairiehomestead.com: A blog focused on homesteading, frugality, and simple living.

Tools:

- **Trello:** trello.com: An organizational tool to help you manage projects, tasks, and ideas.
- **Google Keep:** keep.google.com: A note-taking app for keeping track of shopping lists, DIY project plans, and more.

- **Pinterest:** pinterest.com: A platform for discovering and saving ideas for DIY projects, home hacks, and recipes.

Worksheets and Templates

Budget Templates:

- **Monthly Budget Planner:** A simple template to help you track your income, expenses, and savings each month.
- **Yearly Financial Goals:** A worksheet to set and track your financial goals for the year, including saving targets and debt repayment plans.

DIY Project Plans:

- **Step-by-Step Instructions:** Detailed plans for DIY projects mentioned in this book, including making homemade pasta, refinishing furniture, and sewing reusable shopping bags.
- **Materials Checklist:** A comprehensive list of materials needed for various DIY projects to help you stay organized and prepared.

Frugality Trackers:

- **Savings Tracker:** A visual tracker to monitor your savings progress and keep you motivated.
- **Waste Reduction Log:** A worksheet to record your waste reduction efforts and track the impact of your eco-friendly practices.

"Frugal Living and Productivity Tips: Volume 2"

Continue Your Journey to Financial Freedom and Sustainable Living!

Building on the success of Volume 1, "Frugal Living and Productivity Tips: Volume 2" brings you 25 more invaluable tips to enhance your frugal living journey. This volume dives deeper into creative DIY projects, smart resource management, and eco-friendly practices that will save you money and simplify your life.

What You'll Find in This Volume:

- Innovative home and garden hacks for maximum savings
- Delicious, budget-friendly recipes and kitchen tips
- Smart shopping strategies to avoid impulse buying
- Eco-conscious practices for a greener lifestyle

Actionable Advice and Real-Life Success Stories: Each chapter is filled with practical advice, real-life examples, and clear instructions to help you seamlessly integrate these tips into your daily routine. From making your own pasta to creating a compost heap, you'll find countless ways to enhance your frugality and productivity.

Transform Your Life with Simple, Sustainable Choices: Join the growing community of individuals who are choosing to live smarter, more sustainable lives. "Frugal Living and Productivity Tips: Volume 2" is your guide to continuing this rewarding journey and achieving greater financial and personal freedom.

www.ingramcontent.com/pod-product-compliance
Lightning Source LLC
Chambersburg PA
CBHW071958210526
45479CB00003B/980